Teenage Toss Up

Mom   Dad

Caiden Antonio Drayton

Teenage Toss up:

Stuck Between Two Worlds

by

Caiden Antonio Drayton

Teenage Toss Up:

Stuck Between Two Worlds

ISBN: 979-8-9946037-0-3

Independently Published by

No Handouts Publishing, LLC.

Printed in the United States of America

Edited and Formatted by Tony Drayton

Dedication

For every kid who's ever been stuck in the middle —

between homes, between choices, between voices.

This is for the ones learning to stand tall,

to speak their truth, and to love both sides of their

story.

To my dad — thank you for showing me strength,

realness, and how to use my voice.

To my mom — thank you for your love, your patience,

and your heart.

And to every kid like me —

you don't have to choose sides to know who you are.

— Caiden

Table of Contents

Chapter 1 – The Tossup Begins

Every morning I get up, get fresh, and try to look good for school. That's kind of my thing — I like to walk in looking like I got it together, even when I don't. My dad always says, "How you look is how you feel," so I make sure I'm clean, got my fit right, and my shoes matching. I take about a five- or ten-minute walk to the bus stop. Sometimes I ride the bus, sometimes I just zone out and walk slow, listening to music and thinking about life.

School's whatever, honestly. Some classes are boring, and sometimes I get bored really easy. Not because I don't care, but because it's not challenging. I already get the point before the teacher even finishes explaining it. So, I just sit there, doodling in my notebook or thinking about the weekend. People at school call me "the fly kid," and I guess they're right — I like my style. I don't talk a whole lot in class, but people still notice me.

When I'm at school, I don't really let people in like that.

Nobody really knows what's going on with my parents. I keep that part of my life to myself. It's not that I don't trust my friends — I just don't feel like talking about it all the time. Some things are better left unsaid.

My mom and dad don't really talk much anymore. When they do, it's either quick or it turns into an argument. Sometimes they just ignore each other completely. I've gotten used to it, but that doesn't mean I like it. It's weird, watching two people who raised you act like they don't even know each other. They both do their own thing when it comes to me, and I just kind of go with the flow. I'm chill about it now — not mad, not sad, just tired of it.

My dad though — he's that dude. For real. That's my guy. Me and him, we got this thing where we compete about everything. Who can shoot better in basketball, who's quicker, who knows more about music. He says I cheat, but that's just because I win most of the time. We take trips out of town sometimes, go to movies, or hit hockey games and other sports. He's into old-school hip hop — like the kind where the beats sound dusty — and I'm more into new stuff, but we still clown each other about it. That's our thing. He makes me laugh, but he also teaches me how to handle life.

My mom's different. She's softer — calmer. I know she loves me, even though we don't really do as much as me and my dad do. When I'm at her house, she asks about my day, makes sure I've eaten, and then goes off to do her own thing. It's not bad, just... quiet. Sometimes I wish she'd do more, but I know she's trying in her own way.

So yeah, I live between two worlds. My dad's world is fun and full of energy — like we're always moving. My mom's world is still and quiet, like everything's waiting to happen. And me? I'm somewhere in the middle, trying to figure out which one I belong to more.

I don't tell anybody how it feels — not my friends, not my teachers. Some people think they understand, but they don't. They don't get what it's like to pack your stuff every week, switch houses, and pretend it's normal. It's not. It's just what I've gotten used to.

Sometimes I wonder if things will ever change — like maybe one day they'lltalk without arguing, or maybe they'll both show up at the same game and actually say hi.

But for now, I just do my thing. Go to school, hang with my friends, spend time with both of them, and try not to overthink it.

This whole thing — my life, this back-and-forth — it's a tossup. Some days are good, some days are trash, and most days I'm just in the middle, trying to stay balanced.

But that's the thing about being tossed up — you either spin out of control or you figure out how to land.

And I plan on landing on my feet.

Chapter 2 – Dad Days

When I'm with my dad, life just feels lighter. Like,
I can breathe more. He'sthe type that makes regular days
feel like something's happening, even if we're just chilling.
Sometimes we'll wake up early on a Saturday, and before I
can even grab my phone, he's already saying, "Let's roll." I
never know where we're going — could be the barbershop,
could be an art museum, could be a trip out of town just
because he found a deal on tickets. He's spontaneous like
that. I act like it annoys me sometimes, but I secretly like it.
It keeps things interesting.

My dad's big on teaching me things without making it
sound like a lesson. Like, he'll point at a building or a
mural and start talking about the history behind it — who
painted it, why it matters. He says I need to know about
where I come from, not just where I'm going. One time we
went to this African American history museum, and he
walked me through every section like he'd been there a

hundred times. He told me stories about inventors, artists, and leaders I never even heard of at school. It made me think — like, why don't they teach us this stuff more often? We talk about art too. He says art is power — that it's not just about what you see, it's about what it makes you feel. I never really cared about art before, but when he explains it, it clicks. He says I've got an eye for things, that I notice details other people miss. I don't know if that's true, but I like hearing him say it. He always tells me, "You got potential, man. You just don't see it yet."

That's one thing about my dad — he sees me. Not just the kid version, but like, me. The person I'm becoming. He'll challenge me, mess with me, push me, but it's all love. We're always competing — basketball, video games, who can spot the cleanest sneakers first. I think I'm better at everything, but he swears I cheat. We've been arguing about who's the better shooter since forever.

Music is another thing we go back and forth on. He's stuck

on old-school hip hop — Nas, Rakim, Tribe Called Quest. I'll play new stuff, and he'll act like it's noise. But sometimes I'll catch him nodding his head a little, pretending he's not feeling it. We'll be riding with the windows down, him talking about how lyrics used to mean something, and me saying, "Man, you just old." It'sfunny because those are the moments when we're closest — just talking, joking, vibing.

But it's not all just fun and jokes. My dad's the type who teaches you things in ways you don't forget. Like when I mess up, he doesn't just yell — he'll sit me down and make me think about it. He'll say, "What did you learn from it?" And at first, I'll be annoyed, but later I'll realize he was right. He doesn't baby me, but he doesn't give up on me either.

He's also big on talking about being a young Black man. He tells me the world's not always fair, but that doesn't mean I should ever doubt who I am. He says my voice matters — that I can't just go along with what everybody else says. "You gotta know yourself before the world tries to tell you who you are," he told me once when we were driving home from a trip. I didn't say much back, but I thought about that the whole night.

That's what I like about being around him — it's not fake. He doesn't just say he cares; he shows it. He takes time to actually teach me stuff — not just school stuff, but life stuff. And even when we're clowning each other, I know he's proud of me.

Sometimes I look at him and think, "Yeah, that's what being real looks like." He's not perfect — he's got his moods, his ways, his little speeches that go on too long. But even when he's on my nerves, I know he's trying to make me better. And the truth is, he is.

Every time I leave his house, I feel different — like I learned something without realizing it. He'll dap me up, look me in the eye, and say, "Go be great, son." I laugh it off, but deep down, I feel that. Because when my dad says something like that, it sticks.

And that's the thing about Dad Days — they don't just end when I go back to Mom's. They stay with me. In my head. In how I think. In how I move.

It's like every lesson, every trip, every laugh is a piece of who I'm becoming.

And I wouldn't trade that for nothing.

Chapter 3 – Mom's World

Being at my mom's house is… different. Not bad, just different. Everything's softer, quieter. She lights candles that smell like vanilla or flowers, plays R&B music in the background, and the house always feels warm. She's got a certain way of doing things — like, everything has to be clean, the couch pillows have to be straight, and no shoes on the carpet. When I walk in, she always says, "Hey, baby," and gives me a hug like she hasn't seen me in years, even if it's only been a few days.

I love my mom. For real. She's sweet, and she's always checking on me — asking how school is, if I've eaten, if I need anything. But sometimes it feels like that's as far as it goes. Like, she wants to make sure I'm okay, but she doesn't really see what's going on inside me. I'll tell her, "Yeah, school's fine," or "I'm good," just to keep things simple. I don't like to stress her out, and I don't really think she wants to hear the whole story anyway.

The thing is, she's got this new boyfriend now. I try to be cool about it — I really do. But it's weird. He tries to act friendly, like cracking jokes or asking about school, but it doesn't feel real. It feels like he's doing it because she told him to. You can tell when somebody's heart isn't really in it. It's like he'schecking boxes instead of actually wanting to know me.

I don't say anything though. I just nod, smile, and keep it moving. I don'twant to mess things up for my mom. She seems happy with him, and she deserves that. I can see it in her eyes — she's been through a lot, and she finally looks like she's got something good going. So, I bite my tongue. Even when it feels awkward, I let it slide.

Sometimes I sit in my room at her house and just think. It's quiet — too quiet sometimes. No jokes, no random music debates, no surprise road trips. Just stillness. I'll scroll on my phone or play Xbox, but it's not the same vibe. It'slike her house is all order and calm, but I can't really be myself there. I feel like I gotta walk on eggshells sometimes, like I can't say too much or act too chill or laugh too loud.

One time, she asked me straight up, "You like him?" I wanted to tell her how I really felt — that he's okay, but I don't trust him like that. That I don't feel like he really cares to know me. But when I looked at her, she was smiling, waiting for me to say something good. So, I just said, "Yeah, he's cool." And she smiled even bigger, like that was all she needed to hear. I didn't want to take that away from her.

That's the hard part about being at my mom's. I love her, but I don't feel like I can be 100% honest. Not because she'd be mad — but because I don't want to hurt her feelings. She already carries enough. So, I hold it in.

But sometimes, when I'm lying in bed, I think about how different it feels between her world and my dad's. With my dad, I can say whatever's on my mind — good or bad — and he listens. With my mom, I have to read the room, make sure my words don't mess up the peace.

Still, she's my mom. She raised me, took care of me, and never gave up on me. Even if she doesn't always understand what's going on in my head, I know she loves me. That's why I never disrespect her or snap back. She'sdoing her best, even if sometimes her best feels like distance.

When I think about it, maybe that's what Mom's world is all about — love that's quiet, love that's careful, love that doesn't always say the right thing, but still tries.

And even though I wish I could tell her everything, for now, I'll just keep it cool. Because sometimes, keeping the peace means holding your truth until you're ready to speak it.

Chapter 4 – The Pressure

Some people always got something to say. They act like they know everything about my life just because they've seen bits and pieces of it. Like, they see me with my dad and think they can judge him off a few moments. They say stuff like, "Your dad's a little too chill," or "You need more structure," or "Your mom's probably better for you." But they don't know what they're talking about. They don't see what really happens when it's just me and him.

It used to bother me a little when I'd hear stuff like that. Not because I believed it, but because I didn't like people talking about him like that. My dad might not be perfect, but nobody is. He's real, and that's more than I can say about some of the people who think they got it all figured out.

The truth is, I don't ever question how I feel about my dad. Not once. He'sbeen solid since day one. He shows up, spends time, listens, and actually teaches me things that matter. Some people might not see it, but I don't need them to. I know who my dad is, and that's enough.

Sometimes I can tell people are trying to get me to agree with their opinions — like they want me to say something bad just so they can feel right. But I don't play that game. I just nod, smile, and keep my thoughts to myself. Because I know if I open my mouth, I'm gonna say something that makes them uncomfortable. People don't like hearing the truth when it doesn't fit their story.

When I'm with my dad, none of that outside noise matters. We laugh, we compete, we talk about life. He doesn't try to be somebody else — he's just him. Real, raw, and sometimes stubborn, but always there. That's what I respect most.

He tells me, "Son, people gonna talk. You just make sure you keep being you." That sticks with me. Because no matter what people say about him or even about me, I know the truth about who we are. I don't need to explain it or prove it.

My dad's more than just my parent — he's my best friend. We can clown each other one minute and talk about serious stuff the next. He pushes me when I'm slacking, but he also lets me be myself. That balance — that realness — that's what keeps us close.

Sometimes I wish people would just mind their business. Like, why does everyone feel the need to pick sides? I love both my parents. I don't need anyone telling me who's better. That's between me, my mom, and my dad — not the world.

So yeah, the pressure's there. People talk, people assume. But I don't fold under it. I've learned how to just stay quiet and let my actions speak. Because one thing my dad always says is, "The truth don't need defending. It just needs to be lived."

And that's what I'm doing — living it.

Chapter 5 – The Lessons

Life's funny like that. You think one person's gonna teach you everything, and then you realize it comes from different places — different people, different vibes, different ways. That's how it is with my parents.

My dad teaches me to be bold. To speak up. To know my worth. Every trip we take, every random debate, every competition, he's showing me that I'mcapable of more than I even think. Sometimes it's subtle, like pointing out something in a museum or talking about history. Other times, it's loud — like when we argue about who's the better shooter in basketball. But it all adds up. He makes me realize I can take on the world, even if the world thinks I'm too young to know anything.

My mom teaches me patience and care. She shows me how to love quietly, how to notice the little things that make someone feel valued. She asks about my day, checks in on me, and makes sure I'm fed and okay. That's not flashy or loud, but it matters. I've started to notice that what she does, even if it's subtle, teaches me to respect people, think before I speak, and appreciate the quiet moments.

Both of them teach me in their own ways, and honestly, that's a blessing. Not many kids get that. Some kids only have one parent around, or maybe one parent really doesn't care. I've got two people who love me, even if they show it differently. That's the lesson right there — love doesn't have to look the same to be real.

I've learned to pick up the pieces that matter from each of them. From my dad, I take confidence and courage. From my mom, I take patience and understanding. Put them together, and it starts to shape me. I start to see the person I want to be, the things I want to chase, and how I want to treat people along the way.

Even in the moments where things get messy — like switching houses, or dealing with my mom's boyfriend, or hearing people talk about my dad — I'm learning. I'm learning how to handle it. How to stay chill when things don'tmake sense. How to keep my own mind and my own voice in a world that keeps trying to tell me what to think. I guess the biggest thing I've learned is this: it's okay that my parents are different. It's okay that their ways of showing love aren't the same. They'reboth teaching me lessons that I'm going to use the rest of my life. And that'sthe kind of stuff that sticks — lessons you don't forget, lessons that make you more than just a kid stuck in the middle.

Because of them, I've started seeing who I really am. Not just Tristan, the kid bouncing between houses, but Tristan, the kid who's learning how to stand on his own, think for himself, and live his truth.

And that feels pretty good.

Chapter 6 – Finding My Voice

Ever since I was little, my dad's always told me, "Use your voice. Don't let anybody speak for you." At first, I didn't really get it. I thought he meant talking back or arguing, but it's way deeper than that. It's about knowing who you are, standing up for yourself, and sharing your truth — even when it's hard.

Writing this book? That's me using my voice. I'm not doing it to make anyone mad or to prove anything. I'm doing it because I have something real to say — about my life, my parents, and how it feels to be stuck between them without losing myself. I'm telling my story the way it happened, not the way people think it should have happened.

All the stuff my dad taught me — how to compete, how to laugh, how to see the good in myself — it's in here. And all the stuff my mom taught me — how to love quietly, how to be patient, how to notice the little things — it's in here too.

Those lessons don't cancel each other out. They mix together, and that'swhat makes me… me.

It's weird, but kind of amazing, to realize that being stuck in the middle wasn't just chaos. It was learning. Every trip with my dad, every quiet moment with my mom, every switch between houses — all of it taught me something. It taught me how to think for myself. How to stand on my own. How to see love in more than one way.

Some people might never get it. They might not understand how you can love both parents, even if they're different, without choosing sides. But that's not my problem. My voice isn't for them. It's for me. It's for every kid who's in the middle and doesn't know how to speak up. It's proof that you can have your own truth, even when life tries to tell you otherwise.

So yeah, I'm Tristan. I'm thirteen. I'm stuck between two houses sometimes, but I'm not stuck in life. I've got lessons, I've got love, I've got a dad who pushes me, a mom who cares quietly, and a voice that I'm finally

learning to use.

And that's just the beginning.

Closing – Standing on My Own

Being stuck in the middle hasn't been easy. Some days I feel like I'm carrying the weight of everyone's opinions, expectations, and moods. But I've learned that being stuck doesn't mean being powerless. It means learning how to balance, how to grow, and how to find your own way.

I've got two parents who love me in different ways — one loud and full of energy, one quiet and careful. Both of them show me what it means to care, to push, and to guide someone. Both of them teach me lessons I'll carry for the rest of my life.

The hardest part is learning that I don't have to choose between them. I can love both, respect both, and learn from both. And I can do it without anyone else deciding what that looks like. That's my voice, my life, my truth.

I'm Tristan. Thirteen years old. Figuring out the middle, learning from the edges, and standing on my own. And I know this — no matter what happens, I'll always have the

lessons, the love, and the voice to guide me.

This is me. This is my story. And it's only the beginning.

The End...........Until High School